Inspirations About Love

BOOKS and AUDIOCASSETTES
by BARBARA De Angelis, Ph.D.

Books

Are You the One for Me?
*Confidence: Finding It and Living It
How to Make Love All the Time
*Inspirations About Love
*101 Ways to Transform Your Love Life
  (flip book)
Real Moments
Real Moments for Lovers
Secrets About Men Every Woman
  Should Know

Audiocassettes

*Finding Love
*Confidence: Finding It and Living It
*Making Relationships Work
*Making Love Work

(All of the above are available at your local bookstore. Items marked with an asterisk may also be ordered by calling Hay House at 800-654-5126.)

Inspirations About Love

Barbara De Angelis, Ph.D.

Hay House, Inc.
Carlsbad, CA

Published and distributed in the United States by: Hay House, Inc., P.O. Box 5100, Carlsbad, CA 92018-5100
(800) 654-5126

Edited by: Jill Kramer

Designed by: Christy Allison

Library of Congress Cataloging-in-Publication Data

De Angelis, Barbara.
      Inspirations about love / Barbara De Angelis.
          p. cm.
      ISBN 1-56170-278-1 (trade paper)
BF575.L8D365 1996
152.4'1—dc20
                                            95-46388
                                               CIP

ISBN 1-56170-278-1

00 99 98 97 96   5 4 3 2 1
First Printing, January 1996

Printed in the United States of America

Dear Reader,

This book is filled with ideas and information about love designed to inspire you or someone you care about. I believe that intimate relationships are our greatest blessing and, at the same time, our most challenging and relentless teachers, as they strive to open our hearts and teach us to live as more loving, compassionate human beings. And while we travel the path of love, it's comforting to have some reminders along the way to keep us focused on our purpose and to help us hold our vision.

I offer you this book as a reminder of love's gifts and, hopefully, as a key to love's secrets, so your own journey can be more joy-filled. Use it to inspire yourself and your lover, and if you enjoy its messages, pass them on by giving *Inspirations About Love* to the people you love. *And if you ever need some guidance or clarity, close your eyes, hold the book in your lap, focus your mind on the problem or issue that concerns you, and then open the book randomly to a page, and read the message the Universe has chosen for you.*

Wishing you love always,
Barbara

Love is a force more formidable than any other. It is invisible—it cannot be seen or measured, yet it is powerful enough to transform you in a moment, and offer you more joy than any material possession could.

Most people put more time and effort into deciding what kind of car or video player to buy than they do into deciding whom to have a relationship with. Is it any wonder, then, that our relationships don't turn out the way we want them to?

When you love deeply, courageously,
and with commitment, you invite
Truth into your relationship.

A relationship is the best
seminar in town.

Sharing words of love is one of the
simplest ways for lovers to create
instant real moments.

When you consciously deal with
conflict, that conflict becomes a gift,
not a detriment, to your relationship.

Love always starts with *you*. It is a choice that you make, from moment to moment, to look for what is lovable about your partner.

Love's greatest gift is its ability to make everything it touches sacred.

Lovemaking is not a journey to someplace, but an expression of a place you and your partner *already inhabit* together.

Each time you achieve a new
level of love and intimacy in your
relationship, a new level of
repressed feelings may surface,
ready to be healed by
that new love.

By telling the truth about your needs
to yourself and to others, you will
bring love into your life.

People who go on emotional
rescue missions often mistake
sympathy for love.

When you make a commitment
to a relationship, you invest your
attention and energy in it more
profoundly because you now
experience *ownership* of
that relationship.

Just as worlds build bridges between
your mind and the mind of your
lover, it is touch that builds bridges
between your bodies, and allows you
to have a physical experience of the
invisible energy you feel in your
hearts, the energy we call "love."

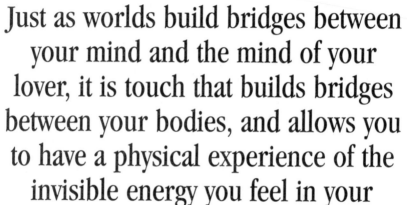

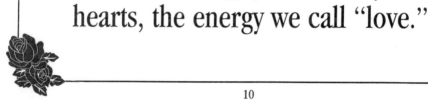

No matter what age you are, or what your circumstances might be, you are special, and you still have something unique to offer. Your life, because of who *you* are, has meaning.

The more connections you and your lover make, not just between your bodies, but between your minds, your hearts, and your souls, the more you will strengthen the fabric of your relationship, and the more real moments you will experience together.

When you stop and pay attention to holy moments and everyday miracles, you will start living with awe and wonder, and start participating in a Divine love affair with God.

The journey in between what you
once were and who you are now
becoming is where the dance
of life really takes place.

Whenever you're sharing love,
you're living your Purpose.

What allows us, as human beings, to psychologically survive life on earth, with all of its pain, drama, and challenges, is a sense of purpose and meaning.

When you let go of your judgments
and create a moment of connection
with another person, you take the
first step toward being truly
compassionate.

Love and kindness are never wasted.
They always make a difference. They
bless the one who receives them,
and they bless you, the giver.

Marriage is not a noun; it's a verb. It isn't something you get, it's something you do. It's the way you love your partner every day.

Speak your truth—it will always lead you back home to yourself.

If you want people to love you for what's inside you and not just for what they see on the outside, you must be willing to do the same for them.

Having healthy relationships with people means loving them for what they are now, not for what you hope they will be like tomorrow.

When you understand why you've made the love choices you have, you will then be free to make new and better love choices.

Love isn't like fat or cholesterol—
there is no need to limit our con-
sumption of it, no sense in assuming
that less love is better than
more love.

When your partner looks at you with a loving gaze, you will feel more completely loved than if you were given any gift, more perfectly beautiful than if any words were spoken, for the silence creates a sacred space in which you can receive love in its purest form.

When you focus on your partner's lack of beauty, your eyes become the enemy of your loving relationship.

The more anger toward the past you carry in your heart, the less capable you are of loving in the present.

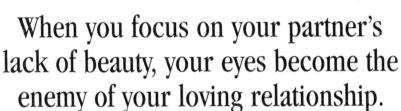

The words you share when you make
love, turn on your brain and help
it turn on your body.

Great love will probably make you
uncomfortable, as it forces you to
look into the mirror at yourself.

If you aren't good at loving yourself,
you will have a difficult time loving
anyone, since you'll resent the time
and energy you give another person
that you aren't even giving
to yourself.

One of the most important ways to make love work for you in your relationship is learning how to communicate the Complete Truth.

Keeping the magic alive in your
relationship means learning how to
fall in love with your partner over
and over again.

All love is an out-of-body experience.
Every true experience of love is
spiritual, as your spirit touches the
spirit of someone or something else.

You don't develop courage by being happy in your relationships every day. You develop it by surviving difficult times and challenging adversity.

Only when your consciousness is totally focused on the moment you are in can you receive whatever gift, lesson, or delight that moment has to offer.

Expressing appreciation for your partner means demonstrating your love verbally, telling your partner what you love about her, and letting her know what she has done that has made you proud.

By healing your negative feelings toward your former partner, you will not carry those feelings into your next relationship.

Some of the most profound real moments that you and your lover can share will happen when you begin to really look into each other's eyes.

You have to know how to be intimate with yourself first before you can be intimate with someone else.

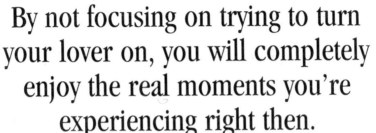

By not focusing on trying to turn your lover on, you will completely enjoy the real moments you're experiencing right then.

You can never feel truly loved if you don't let others see who you really are inside.

The greatest gift you and your partner can give your children is the example of an intimate, healthy, and loving relationship.

Intimacy occurs when the boundaries between you and someone else melt, and your hearts touch.

The purpose of a relationship is to help you heal everything that is not loving *about* you and *in* you.

Difficult times always create
opportunities for you to experience
more love in your life.

If you don't have a vision of where
you want your relationship to go,
it won't go anywhere.

When you learn how to stop hiding
from real moments, you'll find that
they are happening all around you,
and can offer themselves when you
least expect it.

Sometimes the end of a relationship can be the greatest wake-up call of your life because it forces you to take a look at who you are and where you're going.

Often, we don't recognize real moments of happiness in our lives because we've been expecting something different—something bigger, flashier, and more dramatic.

The greater your unresolved fear of
abandonment, the more you may
tend to be excessively needy
and clingy with the partners
in your life.

Strangers can be very pure mirrors of truth, reflecting back to you whatever you've been needing to see, delivering cosmic messages you've been needing to hear.

Needing others is *not* a mistake.
Giving up your responsibility for
satisfying your needs *is* a mistake.

You never lose by loving.
You always lose by holding
back love.

Most communication problems with your partner stem from communicating only part of the truth, not the Complete Truth.

You cannot selectively suppress feelings. The only way to suppress a feeling is to suppress your ability to feel. When you decide to feel again, those same old suppressed feelings will pop up again.

Being naked isn't about taking off
your clothes—it's about taking off
your mask and revealing the feelings
at the core of who you are.

You will have difficulty knowing what you want and need in a partner if you haven't taken the time to get to know yourself.

When you learn to remain fully in the
moment, opening yourself to the
powerful energies dancing between
you and your partner, lovemaking
becomes a continually
orgasmic process.

When you're having an argument with your partner, you're never fighting for the reason you think. You're fighting because you're not feeling loved, supported, or understood by this person.

When you touch your partner with
reverence, silently remind yourself:
*"My purpose is not to turn my
partner on. My purpose is to love
her right now, in this moment."*

The key to choosing the right partner
is to look for a person with good
character, not simply a good
personality.

Each realization you have about mistakes you've made in the past opens the door for you to make more enlightened choices in the future. Instead of being *hopelessly* romantic, you can be *hopefully* romantic.

When we bring enough love into
the darkness, it will illuminate
our hearts with light and
soothe our pain.

To conquer an emotional wound,
you must heal it; and to heal it,
you must feel it.

We need to find the courage to say NO to the things and people that are not serving us if we want to rediscover ourselves and live our lives with authenticity.

There are moments in which the usual boundaries that appear to separate us from one another are penetrated, and in that connection, a kind of magic occurs. We usually call this experience of melting boundaries "love."

To feel "in love," you and your partner must both be in the state of love within yourselves. Only then can you see love in one another.

When you are truly in touch with
your own goodness, you will find
that it naturally overflows, just as
a full river overflows onto the
riverbank. It is fullness that makes
a relationship work, not emptiness.

Having a magical relationship won't happen just because you're in love. You have to work to make the magic keep happening.

When we spend our lives preparing for the future, rather than enjoying the present, we end up postponing happiness. We lose our ability to appreciate and experience joy, so when we do have the opportunity for real moments, we miss them.

The time to tell the people you care about how much you love and need them is *now*, while they're still around to appreciate it.

If you find that you're pushing love out of your life, it may not be that you're afraid of love, but of the loss of love. You consciously or unconsciously avoid love itself in anticipation of the hurt you will feel if you lose it.

Showing affection means giving physical intimacy—touching, holding, being physically close together. It will help connect you and your partner emotionally by linking you on the physical dimension first.

Love is the greatest magic there is.
If you can understand how to make
love work *for* you and not against
you, then *you* become a
great magician.

When you and your partner stop
waiting for the other to start loving,
and just choose to love the other
first, your relationship will
begin to feel full and flowing.

It takes emotional courage to look at
yourself and your relationships and
be willing to change what you
aren't happy with.

The passionate kiss stands alone, even above intercourse, as an act in which both lovers are equally open to one another. You may think you're just kissing, but in truth, your souls are breathing together.

Loving your partner means using words to help him know you and love you better. Don't let your fear or lack of ability be an excuse for not learning how to use words to be a better lover.

The most important sexual technique
I can teach you is to be willing to
love completely and be loved from
the heart. Great sex will follow.

Marriage is a way of loving,
honoring, and celebrating your
partner day by day as an expression
of your commitment to
one another.

The more you love yourself, the less you'll allow others to mistreat you.

When you are embraced with love, the child within you can emerge.

Love can be your doorway
to the Divine.

It's not enough to know *where* to
touch your partner...you have to
know *how* to touch him.

Your relationship should be a place
you often retreat to, not a place
you run from.

Within the sacred circle of your
lover's arms, you can find healing,
wholeness, and redemption.

The real act of marriage takes place in the heart, not in the ballroom or church or synagogue. It is a choice you make—not just on your wedding day, but over and over again—and that choice is reflected in the way you treat your husband or wife.

Sex is a sacred sharing—it is the
way your spirit and the spirit of your
beloved can dance together
in the flesh.

Relationships are an instant and continual training ground. Every day and night, they give you an opportunity to practice love, to stretch yourself beyond what is comfortable, and to keep doing it better.

Finding love in the darkness is simple. Reach out to others when you're in despair, and they will reach back. Say *"I need help,"* and miraculously, help will appear.

When you have a lover in your life,
you are richly blessed. You have
been given the gift of another
person who has chosen to
walk beside you.

Sex, as it ought to be, starts where your bodies unite, and ends where your souls dance, in a place where there is no ending.

You will be amazed to discover how much control you have over the amount of love you give out and the amount of love that comes into your life.

When you are with your lover, the more you relax and feel yourself right there, totally in the moment, the easier it will be to see into the window of your lover's eyes, and allow her to see into yours, so together, you can discover the sweetness that is your love.

Words stir up the love energy
between you and your partner. Your
feelings are always there in your
heart, but it is the words that give
them movement from silence
into expression.

Healing your heart is part of what intimate relationships are about. The process doesn't take a month or a year, but continues over the life of your relationship. The more safety you feel with your partner, the safer you will feel to bring up old, unhealed traumas.

Some of the most exquisite real moments you and your lover can share together will happen when you begin to explore sex as a *physical celebration of the spiritual.* Where you once experienced pleasure during lovemaking, now you will know true ecstasy.

True commitment transforms a mere partnership into a true union and fills every action in that relationship with meaning.

Happiness is not an acquisition—it is a skill. We do not experience happiness because of what we *get*. We experience happiness because of how we *live each moment*.

Your relationship is just the interaction of two individual people. To change the dynamics of the relationship, either one, or preferably, both, partners have to change.

A healthy sex life builds your self-esteem. When you feel that you are a good lover and are desired by your partner, your sense of self-worth increases.

Loving is the only way to get
good at *loving*.

It's not love that hurts—it's when
you stop loving that hurts.

Like an artist molding figures out of clay, your hands, as they touch, give shape and form to your devotion, so that your beloved might know how much he is loved.

Love thrives on connection. It cannot exist without it, for it is *the connection between you and your partner that allows for the flow of love, and that creates the experience of intimacy.*

When you wait for your partner to say something that will *make you* feel more in love, you're setting her up to inevitably disappoint you. *It is not her job to be lovable; it is your job to be loving to her.*

Your eyes cannot lie. How you use your eyes in your relationship can have a positive or negative effect on your partner. You won't have to say anything—he will feel loved or not loved by the way you look at him.

Having sex with someone we love creates more intimacy and closeness between us. Having sex with a partner—especially when we are *making love* and not just having sex—makes us feel special, valued, and cared for.

Each true love we have stretches
our heart in a different direction,
and each relationship serves us
in a different way.

If you are not prepared for the intensity of the powerful learning experience love provides, you will resist your relationship and resent your partner. You will become angry at the mirror (your relationship) for the reflection it is showing you.

Sometimes it takes a tragedy or loss
for us to acknowledge how loved we
truly are by the people in our lives.
This is one of the reasons difficult
times can be rich with real
moments—because they
are rich with love.

Experiencing intimacy with your beloved requires that you open yourself totally to the moment, not just by showing up physically, but by *showing up emotionally.*

The pain you feel in your
relationships helps you to unfold
yourself, to discover the hidden
treasures of spiritual wealth you did
not know existed within you.

You can lie with words, but not with your hands. You cannot fake a loving touch, because *it's not what your hands are doing that makes your partner feel loved*—it's the love you are feeling inside that radiates from your hands.

Words that you speak about yourself
open the door to your spirit so that
your partner can enter and see the
fullness and uniqueness that is you.

Being an emotional refuge for your lover does not mean *fixing* him or solving his problems. It's not about *doing* anything—it's about just *being there* in a real moment of love.

Your ability to feel is a gift, not a curse. Just as your nerves report physical sensations to help keep you safe physically, so too do your feelings tune you in to what you need for emotional health.

Every relationship has its ups and downs, its conflicts and problems. *But every conflict is really an opportunity to grow closer and experience more love.*

Use the energy from your eyes to
adore and caress your partner, to
search out and appreciate all the
everyday wonders he possesses.
Each time you look at your lover,
you will find more reasons to
fall deeper in love.

A truly successful relationship has more than love and compatibility as its foundation—it has direction. Having a direction in your relationship allows *it* to grow, and allows *you* to grow. It is the difference between just *being* together and *becoming* together.

Your intimate relationship is the
most precious gift in your life. It
deserves some time every day to
be celebrated.

Words furnish your feelings with
concrete form so they can be passed
on to your mate. Each expression of
caring, of appreciation, of gratitude
becomes a beautiful present you
offer your beloved.

Instead of assuming that you are an adult who ought to be an expert at love by now, you can give yourself permission to *know nothing* and, therefore, to *learn everything*.

When your relationship is filled with real moments, it will cease to feel like an obligation or burden and, instead, become a healing sanctuary.

The more love and support that you receive from the friends in your life, the less dependent you will be on a mate to fulfill all of your needs.

One of the most certain ways to sabotage your relationship is to believe the romantic myth that says: *"If my partner is the right one for me, if she really loves me, she will automatically know just what I need."* It is up to you to share your needs with your partner.

Don't be in a hurry to *get some-where* during sex. You'll miss the experience of where you are, and you'll never know the real moments of timeless ecstasy that are waiting for you if you'd only pay attention to NOW.

An intimate relationship is a sacred opportunity for you to use love as a path for personal and spiritual transformation. It forces you to open where you were closed, to feel where you were numb, to express what was silent, to reach out where you would retreat.

Loving isn't something you do to get a result—it's an action that, in itself, fills you with joy and therefore fulfills its own purpose at each moment.

To begin learning how to touch with love, you need to understand and appreciate the magic that is contained in your hands. Your hands are not just physical appendages, *they are transmitters of the powerful life energy that flows through your body.*

Emotional openness in a partner gives you access to her inner world. It is this person's way of offering you the key to her heart. It's the true fulfillment of the promise you make when you decide to be together.

Don't wait for your partner to fill you up with love. You need to learn how to continually fall in love with him over and over again.

Love is a positive force: *it thrives in an atmosphere of positivity and starves in an atmosphere of negativity.* That's why it's so important to find a partner who has a positive attitude.

True commitment is a constant state
of awareness of a sacred process
that you and your partner have
entered into together to experience
the highest joys and lessons
that love has to offer.

Your lover offers you an abundance of miracles every day. She is your doorway to Heaven here on Earth.

When you forgive others for their imperfections, you forgive yourself for your own.

When you and your mate forget that your relationship is a gift, when you don't remember to cherish one another, that's when you cease being lovers.

The sharing of the sacred force of sex between you and your partner is a celebration of life and of your relationship. Each time you and your beloved unite, you penetrate each other's physical boundaries, and merge not just your hearts, but your bodies, in the most intimate way possible.

Love is up to you. You have the free-dom to choose whether or not to have a relationship. You also have the freedom to choose to learn how to have a *successful* relationship. You are the only one with the power to do something about your life! Love is up to you.

Love is the greatest turn-on that there is. The energy that is love makes our cells vibrate with delight and makes our souls rejoice.

Your hands hold a magical power.
They can give the passion in your
soul, a voice. They can speak of
things for which there are no words.
They can make your love visible.

An intimate relationship is a guaranteed way of doing some emotional housecleaning. With the right tools, that process of clearing out the old hurts, resentments, and fears can be one of the most exciting adventures of your life!

The act of kissing imitates the act of sexual intercourse—a part of you enters your partner's body, a part of you receives her body into yours.

When you're making love to your partner, the better you get at staying in the moment and the longer you allow the sexual energy to circulate in your body before releasing it, the greater your physical and emotional ecstasy will become.

Love connects you to the power within you. That's why it feels so good to be in love. When you stop loving others, you weaken your connection to your inner power and your ability to love yourself.

When you celebrate your needs,
when you allow yourself to feel and
express them, the more potential for
passion and fulfillment you will
experience in your relationships.

Most of the depression, boredom, and mal-content that people experience in their lives has its source in the suppression of feeling. One big value of staying open to all of your feelings is that *when you can feel, you can heal.* Without feeling, the inner self has no chance to come out and playfully express its genius and brilliance.

Love offers you an opportunity for deep, spiritual awakening, for when you love, the usual boundaries that separate you from something else dissolve; you transcend the illusion of separation that defines human existence, and you experience Oneness.

There is really no right or wrong way to make love. Essentially, sex is "right" when it supports you in feeling good about yourself and the relationship and leaves you with a sense of peace and happiness. It is "wrong" when it adds to your negative feelings about yourself or your partner and leaves you feeling unhappy and disturbed.

When you're making love and you share with your partner on an emotional level, you open the channel for the sexual energy to flow up and be transformed into love energy, thus making room for more sexual energy when the next wave rises.

Love bridges the gap between yourself and the universe around you. *When you are living in love, you no longer live in a world of a million separations, but of a million connections.* You are in a loving relationship with everything.

Offering your marriage to God or a Higher Intelligence for blessing is tremendously empowering. It's a way of honoring your Source for the gift of love you've found in one another, and asking for continued clarity and vision so you can expand that gift.

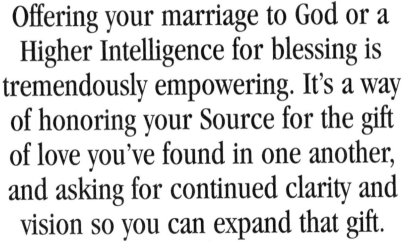

True compatibility in a relationship includes not only the direction you are moving in, but how quickly or slowly you choose to travel.

The challenges and difficulties that
you experience in your relationship
will always illuminate your most
needed lessons.

Finding your ability to feel is the first step toward experiencing true intimacy with your partner and creating real moments in your relationship.

You don't have to wait until you experience an overwhelming feeling of love to share that love with your partner. You can make these gestures because you remember that you love him, and because you know that by choosing to love, you will not only make your partner happy, but you will focus your own attention on the love you feel, and *bring yourself* joy.

Passionate sex is a symptom of a passionate relationship. And a passionate relationship means knowing how to make love with your partner all the time, and not waiting until you get into bed to start.

When you use language that makes your partner feel wrong, you will just make things worse between you. You don't have to blame, condemn, name-call, generalize, or make value judgments— all you have to do is tell your partner how you're feeling.

Learning to master *connection* is one of the keys to making love all the time in your life. Connection creates a feeling of aliveness, energy, creativity, self-esteem, fulfillment, and love. It is the essential ingredient in loving.

Making love is an art and a science, just like preparing a meal or playing an instrument. It takes skill and practice, and daily application of those skills to make it work every day.

Love makes every space sacred, and every moment meaningful. The easiest way to make any space a place where you can experience real moments is to bring love to it.

Love dies in an atmosphere of dishonesty. When you suppress the truth, you destroy your ability to feel. And when you stop feeling, you stop loving.

Falling out of love and losing that magnetic attraction does not happen overnight. It is simply the inevitable result that occurs when one or both of you takes the gift of your partner for granted, when you stop thinking and behaving like lovers.

The difference between being with someone without a commitment and with a commitment is the same as the difference between renting or buying a house.

The areas in which you and your partner experience the greatest conflict in your relationship will be your greatest teachers.

By learning how to use your sexual energy in a conscious way, rather than using it unconsciously, you can turn the sexual experience from one that simply feels good to one that rejuvenates you physically, emotionally, and even spiritually.

The emotional and physical home you and your partner create ought to, at its best, be a haven, *a shelter of positive energy that can offer you courage and clarity, comfort and support whenever life challenges you with difficulties.*

Men and women all want the same things—to feel worthwhile, to feel good about themselves, *and to be loved.*

It doesn't take much courage to simply have a relationship. But it does take courage to love your partner deeply, to not be merely a couple, but to be true lovers, and to walk the path of conscious relationship together.

The more honest, open moments you and your partner spend connecting from the heart, the harder it will be to pretend that things are fine when they're not, to convince yourself that you're being loved enough when you aren't, and to ignore the shadows in your relationship.

When your partner holds you, and you allow yourself to surrender to the love she surrounds you with, you enter a sacred place in which the world around you fades away, and your universe is contained in the space within her arms.

Making new and healthy love
choices changes your emotional
programming by healing your fear
and building new trust.

It is the vision of your relationship as
a transformational path that will give
you and your partner the strength,
patience, and perseverance to travel
the High Road of Love together.

The ability to love is the greatest gift you have been given. When you celebrate the gift of love by living *in love* and living *as love*, you will become the miracle...and the earth will be blessed with peace.

When the channel between you and your partner's heart is unblocked, your spirits can join together at the same time as your bodies become one. Then all of you will be making love, and there will be nothing left between you that is not love. This is sacred communion.
This is ecstasy.

...And one final inspiration about love...

Look around you—you will see people who need your love. Offer it to them. In that moment, you will be their blessing. And God will be smiling....

About the Author

Barbara De Angelis, Ph.D., is an internationally recognized expert on human relations and one of America's most influential teachers in the area of personal and spiritual development. She is the author of six bestselling books: *Real Moments, Real Moments for Lovers, Secrets About Men Every Woman Should Know, Are You the One for Me?, Confidence: Finding It and Living It,* and *How to Make Love All the Time.* Barbara has hosted her own television and radio shows, as well as appearing for several years on CNN as their Newsnight Relationship Expert. Her television infomercial, *MAKING LOVE WORK,* is the most successful relationship program of its kind. Barbara is known for sharing her warmth, vitality, and inspirational presence with her audiences.

We hope you enjoyed this Hay House book.
If you would like to receive a free catalog featuring additional
Hay House books and products, or if you would like information about the Hay Foundation, please write to:

 Hay House, Inc.
P.O. Box 5100
Carlsbad, CA 92018-5100

or call:
(800) 654-5126